P9-BJD-711

Tooth Traditions around the World

The Child's World

Published by The Child's World®
1980 Lookout Drive • Mankato, MN 56003-1705
800-599-READ • www.childsworld.com

Acknowledgments
The Child's World®: Mary Berendes, Publishing Director
Red Line Editorial: Editorial direction
The Design Lab: Design
Amnet: Production

Design elements: Markovka/Shutterstock Images

Photographs ©: Philip Dyer/iStockphoto, Cover, Title; Zurijeta/Shutterstock
Images, 5; Shutterstock Images, 7, 21; Fotocrisis/Shutterstock Images, 9;
iStockphoto, 15; Steffen Foerster Photography/Shutterstock Images, 17;
Pichugin Dmitry/Shutterstock Images, 27

ISBN 9781614734307
LCCN 2012946516

Printed in the United States of America
Mankato, MN
November, 2012
PA02145

About the Author

Ann Malaspina has written books about history, athletes, and animals. She likes to ride her bike, look for rare birds, and bake anything with chocolate. Ann also likes to travel. When she visited Mexico, she learned that ancient Mexicans collected jaguar teeth.

About the Illustrator

Elisa Chavarri is a Peruvian illustrator who works from her home in Alpena, Michigan, which she shares with her husband, Matt, and her cat, Sergeant Tibbs. She has previously illustrated *Fly Blanky Fly*, by Anne Margaret Lewis, and *Fairly Fairy Tales*, by Esmé Raji Codell.

Table of Contents

Chapter One

A Tooth Is Loose!

Losing a baby tooth is a special event. It is a sign of growing up. People have always **celebrated** losing their teeth. Hundreds of years ago, Christian children in England dropped the tooth into a fire and asked God to send a new tooth. Bemba children in Africa threw the tooth to the east and charcoal to the west. They hoped the rising sun would bring a new tooth.

In other places, children asked animals with strong teeth to take the tooth and bring a better one. On the Cook Islands in the Pacific Ocean, children sang, "Big rat! Little rat! Here is my old tooth. Pray give me a new one." In Germany, the tooth was dropped into a mouse hole so the child would not get toothaches.

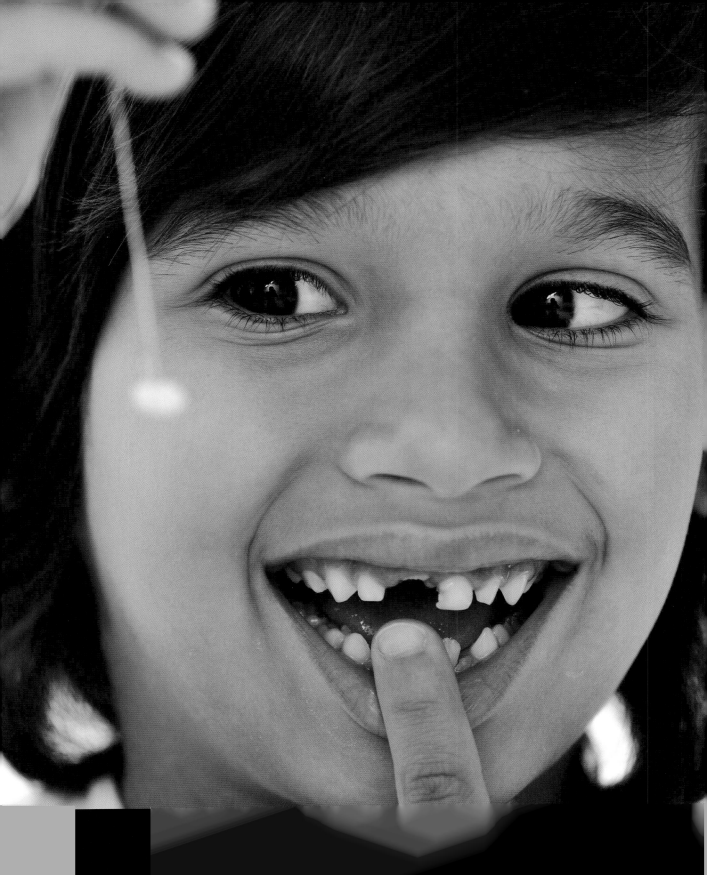

Today, many children in the United States tuck their teeth under a pillow for the tooth **fairy**. Children in Asia toss the tooth on the roof or ground for good luck. Children in the Middle East throw their baby teeth to the sun. Others save the tooth in a box or make jewelry with the tooth!

Babies are born with 20 teeth in their jaws. They are called primary, baby, or milk teeth. Babies' teeth start coming in when they are about six months old. The first teeth might fall out when a child is about six or seven. A new permanent tooth will poke up soon. The 32 permanent teeth have to last a person's whole life. Teeth help people chew, bite, talk, smile, and whistle. It's important to take good care of your teeth!

Chapter Two

The Tooth Fairy

When children in the United States lose a tooth, they put the tooth under their pillow. Then they go to sleep. In the morning, the tooth is gone! In its place is a gift or money. Sometimes there is a note signed by the tooth fairy.

Children write notes to the tooth fairy. Some make a fancy tooth box or slip the tooth into an envelope. Others drop the tooth into a glass of water or on a plate or leave it by the window. The tooth fairy will find it.

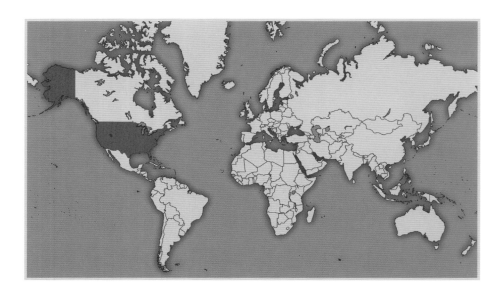

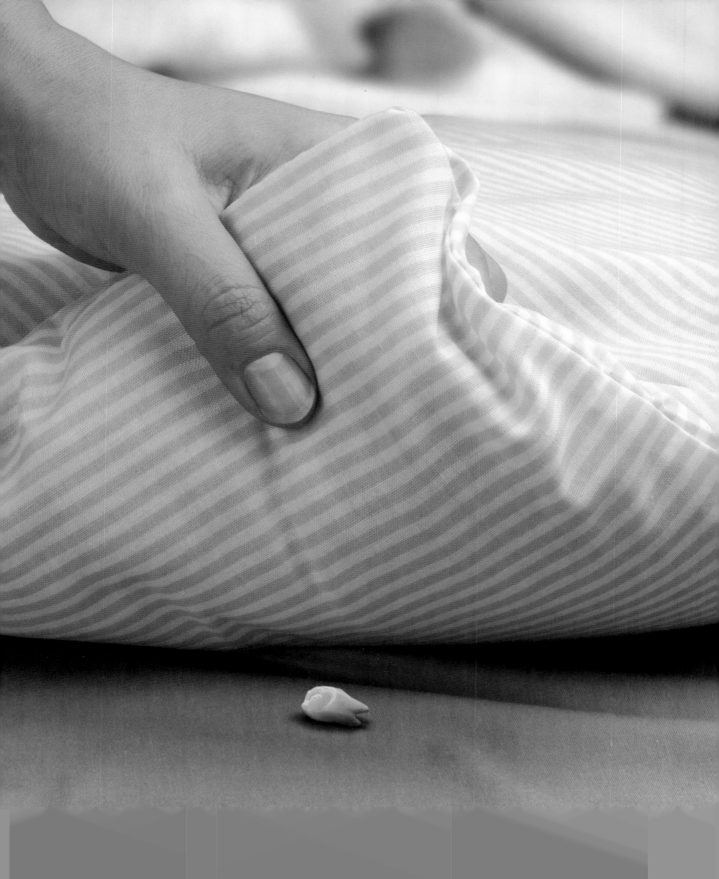

There are many songs, stories, and movies about the tooth fairy. But no one has ever seen the tooth fairy. Most people imagine the tooth fairy is tiny and has wings. She is also strong, kind, and brave. She will go anywhere to find a baby tooth.

In Italy, some children believe in a tooth fairy named *la fatina dei denti* (lah FAH-tee-nah dee DEN-tee). Others think a tooth mouse, witch, or the Christian saint Apollina takes children's lost teeth.

Chapter Three

El Ratón Pérez

Long ago in Spain, a Christian **priest** wrote a story about a mouse. The mouse's name was *El Ratón Pérez* (EL rah-TONE PAY-rez), or "The Mouse Pérez." Pérez lived in a box of cookies under a bakery. At night, he ran through the city to find lost baby teeth.

Pérez wears a red jacket and carries a sword. He has a very long tail. He takes away the tooth and leaves a coin or small gift. Children write notes to him, too. Maybe that's why El Ratón Pérez wears a pair of gold glasses. He wants to read every word.

Today, the brave mouse is loved around the world in places where people speak Spanish. Sometimes he is called *Ratoncito* (rah-tone-SEE-toh), or "Little Mouse." In Mexico, Costa Rica, and Spain, children hide baby teeth under their pillows for Ratoncito to find.

Chapter Four

Strong as a Beaver's Tooth

A Cherokee Indian **tradition** says that when a child loses a baby tooth, she holds it in her hand and runs around the house. "Beaver, put a new tooth into my jaw!" she repeats four times. Then she throws the tooth on the roof. She wants her adult teeth to be as strong as the beaver's.

The beaver is an important animal for the Cherokee. The Cherokee word for beaver is *doya* (DOY-ya). They respect the beaver's strength, especially its strong teeth. The Cherokee word for tooth is *nadohgv* (na-DOH-ga).

The beaver's sharp teeth can gnaw through a hard tree. With its teeth, the beaver picks up logs and sticks. It carries the wood to a stream or pond, where it builds a dam. No wonder Cherokee children want teeth like a beaver's!

Chapter Five

White Tooth of the Gazelle

Some children in northern Africa throw their baby teeth into the sky. They ask for a strong tooth in return. "Here, take the yellow tooth of the donkey and give me the white tooth of a gazelle," they say in Algeria. On the open plains of Africa, gazelles graze in the grasses. Gazelles have striped fur and large ringed horns. They are beautiful and swift.

Many people in northern Africa are **Muslim**. Their religion is Islam. Muslims believe in Allah, which means God in Arabic. When they throw a baby tooth to the sky and sun, Muslim children are also giving a gift to Allah.

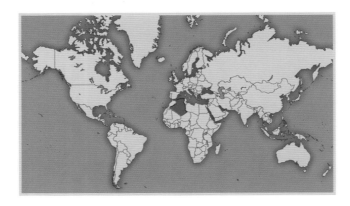

Chapter Six

Up on the Roof

In Japan, families share a special meal about 100 days after a baby is born. It is the *okuizome* (OH-kwi-zoh-meh), or "first meal." They eat sticky rice cakes, grilled red snapper, and vegetables. A stone is also on the food tray. The baby bites the stone and tastes the food. This means she will have strong teeth and always have enough to eat.

When a bottom tooth falls out, a Japanese child takes it outside. He throws the tooth back over his head to the roof. He believes this helps his new tooth grow straight up. Upper teeth are thrown below the house so that they grow down. Children in Greece, China, and many other countries toss their teeth on the roof or over the house.

Chapter Seven

Song for a Magpie

In South Korea, children toss their baby teeth up to the roof. Then they sing a song for a magpie bird. They wish for a magpie to take the old tooth away and bring a new one.

> "Dear magpie, dear magpie.
> Here is my old baby tooth.
> Would you bring me my new tooth?"

The magpie is a member of the crow family. Its wings are black and white. The bird's call is loud and clear. Koreans believe the magpie is a lucky bird that brings good news. A magpie's chatter means a guest is coming soon. The Korean word for magpie is *gga chi* (KAH CHEE).

Chapter Eight

Good Little Mouse

Children in France believe in *la petite souris* (la pa-TEET soo-REE), or "the little mouse." They put their baby tooth under the pillow. While they sleep, the mouse sneaks under the pillow and takes the tooth. She leaves money in its place.

The mouse uses shiny baby teeth to build her castle. In French, a baby tooth is called *dent de lait* (DON du LAY). This means a milk tooth.

The little mouse is from the French folktale "*La Bonne Petite Souris*" (la BUN pa-TEET soo-REE), or "The Good Little Mouse." In the story, a mouse turns into a fairy. The fairy wants to help the good queen defeat a wicked king. The fairy hides under the king's pillow and attacks him at night. In the end, the king dies. The queen and her daughter, the princess, live happily ever after.

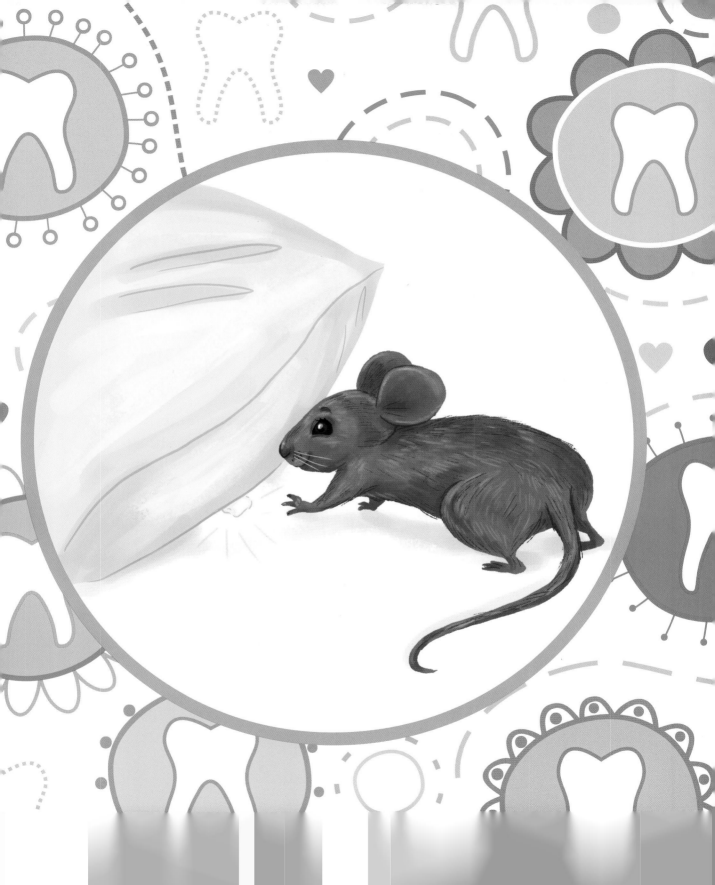

Chapter Nine

Wear a Tooth!

The custom of wearing animal and even human teeth for health or good luck is very old. Today, some people make jewelry from baby teeth. Some believe the teeth will protect them. Others think the tooth is pretty, like a pearl or stone.

People in northeast Brazil make baby teeth **amulets**, or lucky charms. They make a hole in the tooth and thread a red string through it. They wear the necklace to keep away evil.

Queen Victoria of Great Britain lived from 1819 to 1901. She wore a special gold pin. It had a green thistle plant with a white blossom. The blossom was her oldest child's baby tooth.

Chapter Ten

Guardian Dog

Giving a baby tooth to a dog is an old tradition in Mongolia. The family wraps the tooth in bread or meat. Then the dog eats it. Mongolians believe the dog will protect the child. The dog will make sure the new tooth grows in strong.

Dogs are important in Mongolia, where people herd flocks of reindeer, sheep, and yaks. Wolves are the animals' worst enemies. The large Mongolian dogs keep the wolves away, so the herd is safe. To protect their families, the dogs also bark at strangers. Mongolian dogs are respected and not treated as pets.

Pérez the Mouse

This is a retelling of the story of Pérez the Mouse. The priest Louis Coloma wrote it in 1894. He wrote it for King Alfonso XIII of Spain when Alfonso was young. Alfonso's nickname was Bubi.

In Spain, there lived a young king named Bubi the First. One day he was eating his bread and milk. His tooth wiggled. The court doctor tied red silk around it. YANK! Out came the tooth.

That night, Bubi wrote a note to Pérez the Mouse. He put the note and tooth under his pillow. Then he went to sleep. TICKLE. TICKLE. Bubi woke up. A mouse stood on his pillow. He wore a straw hat, red jacket, and gold glasses. A sack of teeth hung on his back. Pérez had arrived!

The mouse was in a hurry. He had to pick up the tooth of a poor boy named Giles. When Bubi sneezed, Pérez turned him into a mouse, too. They slipped down a hole under the bed.

After a long journey, the two mice found Giles's house. It was cold inside. The sleeping boy had no blanket or food. Bubi began to cry. He did not know that people in his kingdom were hungry and cold.

From that day on, Bubi was a kind and generous king. His people were warm and well fed. King Bubi never forgot the night Pérez the Mouse took his tooth and showed him the world.

Make a Tooth Box

A tooth box is a fun way to celebrate a lost baby tooth. Slip the box under a pillow for the tooth fairy or El Ráton Pérez, or keep it in a drawer to save forever.

Materials
small cardboard box
craft glue
paint
two paper plates
small paintbrush
glitter (shiny gems, sparkles)
newspaper

Directions
1. Place newspaper over a flat surface to make a clean work space. Spread glitter on one of the paper plates. Pour a spoonful of craft glue on the other paper plate. Mix a few drops of paint into the glue for color.
2. Use the paintbrush to coat one side of the box with the colored glue. Press the glue side of the box into the glitter. Repeat until all sides of the box are coated except the bottom.
3. Shake the box to remove loose glitter. Use the paintbrush to fill in any empty spots with colored glue and glitter. Let dry.

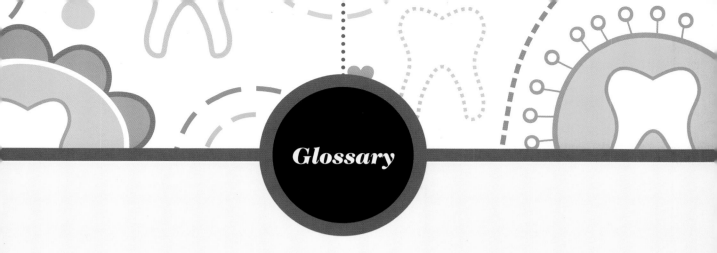

Glossary

amulets (AM-yuh-lates) Amulets are lucky charms. People make amulets with baby teeth.

celebrated (SEL-uh-brate-id) To celebrate is to observe or take notice of a special day. Many people celebrate losing teeth.

fairy (fair-ee) A fairy is an imaginary being with a human form, wings, and magical powers. The tooth fairy takes baby teeth and leaves money or presents.

Muslim (MUHZ-lim) A Muslim is a person who practices the religion of Islam. Muslims believe in Allah.

priest (PREEST) A priest is a clergy member who can lead religious ceremonies. A priest wrote the story of Pérez the Mouse.

tradition (truh-DISH-un) A tradition is a way of thinking or acting communicated through culture. Many people have baby tooth traditions.

Learn More

Books

Colato Laínez, Renae. *The Tooth Fairy Meets El Ratón Pérez*. Berkeley, CA: Tricycle Press, 2010.

Diakité, Penda. *I Lost My Tooth In Africa*. New York: Scholastic, 2006.

Web Sites

Visit our Web site for links about tooth traditions around the world: ***childsworld.com/links***

Note to Parents, Teachers, and Librarians: We routinely verify our Web links to make sure they are safe and active sites. So encourage your readers to check them out!

Index